Becoming The Principal I Never Had

Becoming The Principal I Never Had
Copyright © 2024 by Ron Anthony
All rights reserved.

Published by Parenting Principals Publishing
2808 Cain Dr
Anna, Tx, 75409
https://www.facebook.com/parentingprincipals

ISBN: 9798332093739

No part of this book may be reproduced, stored in a retrieval system, or transmitted in any form or by any means, electronic, mechanical, photocopying, recording, or otherwise, without the prior written permission of the publisher, except for brief quotations used in reviews or scholarly work.

For information, address Parenting Principals Publishing at parentingprincipalshub@gmail.com.

Cover design by Ron Anthony
Interior design by Ron Anthony
Printed in the United States of America

First Edition

Library of Congress Cataloging-in-Publication Data is available upon request.

Disclaimer: The views and opinions expressed in this book are those of the author and do not necessarily reflect the official policy or position of any educational institution or organization.

Becoming The Principal I Never Had

A Journey of Empathy, Leadership, And Transformation

Ron Anthony

This book is dedicated to the thousands of students I have worked with throughout my years in education. As much as you were learning from me, I was learning from you. I am genuinely grateful for a lifetime of memories created together.

Thank you for inspiring me.

This book is also a tribute to my family — my wife Tasha, and our three children, Cameron, Mason, and McKinley - Grace. Keep pursuing your dreams, for you hold the pen to script your own future.

Contents

Introduction

The Genesis of Leadership

- Early Educational Journey
- The Inspiration Behind Becoming a Principal
- Defining the Principal I Aspire to Be

Building Positive Relationships

- Learning Students Names: The Power of Personal Connection
- Finding Common Ground: Fostering Meaningful Conversations
- Deeply Rooted: Mentorship
- Meeting Students Where They Are: The Power of Mentoring / No Judgement

Cultivating a Culture of Belonging

- Making Every Student Feel Important
- Authenticity Beyond the Title: Sharing Personal Stories

Nurturing Growth and Accountability

- Holding Students Accountable: Balancing Support and Expectations
- High Fives, Fist Bumps, and Hugs: Creating a Culture of Affirmation

Empowering Through Support

- Small Group Lunches: Creating Safe Spaces for Dialogue
- Filling in the Gaps: Supporting Basic Needs
- Leading with Compassion: Advocating for Every Student

Making Connections: The Blueprint

- Carpool Line
- Lunch Time Chats
- Classroom Visits
- Hallway Super Star
- A Recess to Remember
- Support Outside of School

Building Lifelong Relationships

Shattered Dreams

The Blessing in Disguise

The Final Bell

Introduction

In the corridors of my childhood schools in Baton Rouge, LA, I often yearned for a connection that never came. My interactions with principals were limited and distant as I don't have any memories of these past school leaders. The only principal I can recall is my middle school principal, Mr. Stevenson, who was known to paddle students who got out of line. This void catalyzed my journey to redefine what it means to be a school principal. "Becoming the School Principal I Never Had" is a testament to the transformative power of relationships and their profound impact on students' lives.

From the outset of my education career, I consciously decided to prioritize building positive relationships with every student. I wanted to be more than just an authority figure who enforces rules; I aspired to be a mentor, a confidant, and a champion for each child's potential. In doing so, I committed to ensuring every student feels loved, heard, and valued within the school community. This book chronicles my evolution from a distant observer to a profoundly engaged leader. It highlights the pivotal moments and experiences that shaped my philosophy and practice as a principal. Through personal stories and practical insights, I illustrate the profound difference that intentional, compassionate leadership can make.

Principals have a unique and powerful opportunity to influence the lives of thousands of students throughout their careers. Our responsibility goes beyond maintaining discipline; we are charged with creating an environment where students can flourish academically, socially, and emotionally. By fostering genuine connections, we can inspire confidence, resilience, and a love for learning in our students.

"Becoming the School Principal I Never Had" is a reflection of my journey and a guide for current and aspiring principals who seek to leave a lasting positive impact. It offers strategies for building meaningful relationships, creating an inclusive school culture, and leading with empathy and vision.

As you turn these pages, I hope you find inspiration and practical advice to help you on your path. This book challenges us to recognize the role of a principal is not confined to the walls of an office but extends into the hearts and minds of every student we encounter. Together, we can transform our schools into places where every child feels valued and empowered to reach their fullest potential.

The Genesis of Leadership

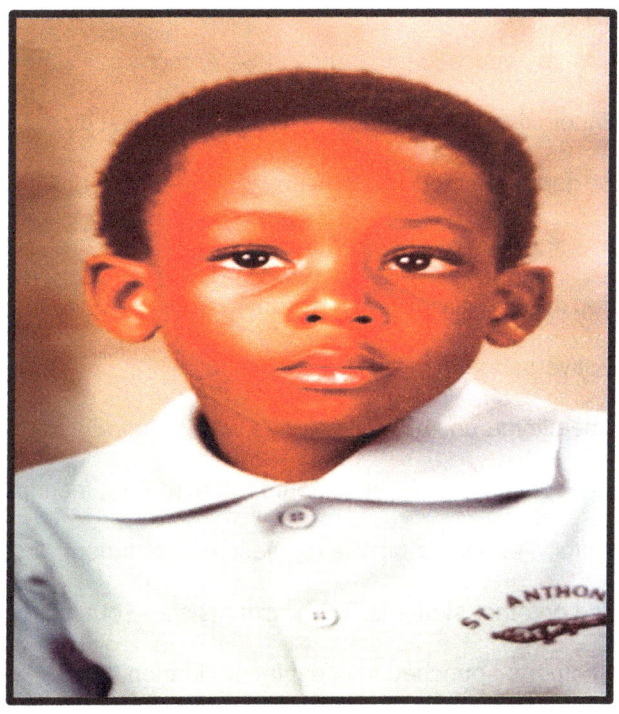

"As school leaders, we must foster a culture where students eagerly anticipate returning to school each day. By creating the right environment, we enable them to truly thrive."

Early Educational Journey

I began my educational journey at St. Anthony's, a school in the inner city of Baton Rouge, Louisiana. My first day of kindergarten memories are vivid: tears streaming down my face, a tight grip on my mother's hand, and a solid reluctance to step into the classroom. That day began a tumultuous but formative period in my early education.

The playground at St. Anthony's was a central part of my childhood. I spent countless hours there, making friends and, regretfully, earning a bit of a reputation as a student who picked on other students. Two incidents stand out sharply in my memory: I punched my best friend, Marlon, in the stomach, and another boy, Michael, suffered even more at my hands—I made his school life miserable daily. My behavior was so problematic that the school called my parents on several occasions. I often wonder if my behavior led my parents to transfer me to another school. Despite the trouble I caused, the face of the Principal at St. Anthony's remains a blank in my memory, a testament perhaps to how disconnected I felt from authority figures during my three years there.

My transition from St. Anthony's to Greenville Elementary marked the end of my private school years, spanning kindergarten through second grade. Greenville was just a five-minute drive from my house, opening a new world of experiences. I attended school for the first time with kids from my neighborhood. The shift from private to public school was initially challenging. In my first school, my misbehavior was glaringly obvious, but at my new school, it paled in comparison to the antics of my new peers. I went from being the student who picked on others to trying to avoid being picked on. Despite the rough start, I fondly remember my time at Greenville. The teachers left a lasting impression, though I can't recall the principal or assistant principal. Their presence was so minimal that getting into trouble was the only way to interact with them.

After finishing elementary school, I moved to Capitol Middle, another neighborhood institution. Having many friends from Greenville slightly eased the transition. However, the first day was nerve-wracking. The school was more prominent and navigating between classes within the five-minute passing periods felt like an impossible challenge. One day, I didn't use the restroom because I was terrified of being late. Adding to my stress was opening a combination lock on my locker. Picture a kid lugging a heavy backpack, trying desperately not to wet his pants—yeah, that was me.

By the time I reached middle school, my behavior had significantly improved. I was no longer the troublemaker. Capitol Middle's Principal, Mr. Stevenson, was memorable, not for building positive relationships with students, but for his reputation as a strict disciplinarian. Seeing a large wooden paddle hanging on his door was enough to keep most of us in line. There were rumors of him taking misbehaving students into a small closet for paddling, though I never experienced it firsthand. Despite his intimidating presence, I thrived at Capitol Middle, earning a spot on the A-Honor Roll each year and playing on the basketball team.

My journey continued to Belaire High School in the fall of 1989. Entering high school as a confident yet naïve teenager, I quickly realized that my academic habits were sorely lacking. English and Biology classes were immediate challenges, and I blamed the teachers for my poor performance. Eventually, I understood that my struggles were due to my lack of effort. On the brighter side, I excelled in History and Algebra I, the latter taught by one of the basketball coaches.

High school life was a mix of freedom and responsibility. Lunchtime was a highlight; I often indulged in nachos and candy from the snack bar. Strangely, I only set foot in the cafeteria during a basketball banquet in my senior year. The experience of seeing a part of the school I had avoided for four years was surreal.

High school also brought less interaction with administrators. We had a head principal and two assistant principals whose primary responsibility seemed to be shouting at students to get to class on time. My first interaction with an administrator was a trip to the office for something I did not do. One of my neighborhood friends cursed out the teacher, but when he arrived at the principal's office, he told the principal his name was Ron Anthony. Without verifying the information or knowing the students, he called my father and told him what had happened. My father leaves work and drives down to the school only to show up in the front office looking at a kid who is not his own. My father politely tells the principal that the kid sitting in the chair is not his son. During this time, I was sitting in class and had no clue what happened until my teacher said my principal wanted to see me because my father was in the office. The walk to the office was probably the longest in history. I played back my entire day in my head as I knew I didn't do anything to warrant my father showing up to the school. I was scared as hell. When I walked in, my father explained the situation, but he said if he and I had crossed paths in the hallway before finding out it was a mix-up, it would not have been good for me. Thank you, God!! This incident underscored a significant issue: the principal didn't know his students well enough to distinguish between them.

    The only other time I interacted with my principal was when he handed me my diploma at graduation. I didn't know it then, but God was laying the foundation for me to "Become the Principal I Never Had."

The Inspiration Behind Becoming a Principal

The idea of becoming a principal was implanted in my mind during the Spring of 2002 at a job fair at my college, Southern University. I met an African American recruiter from Richardson ISD who said if you come to the district, only teach for three years and then go into administration. He reasoned that there was a need for more African American male administrators. At the time, I was not thinking about becoming a school Principal; I only needed a teaching job because I was graduating in a few weeks. I planned to teach and coach, hoping to become a head basketball coach at a high school and win a state championship.

Interestingly, after I accepted a teaching job at Lake Highlands Junior High School in Richardson, Texas, my first principal, Mrs. Burrell, approached me and asked if I was interested in becoming a principal one day. Years ago, a program in Richardson paid for minority teachers to go back to school to receive a master's degree in administration so that they could one day become principals in the district.

Even as she explained the program, I remained determined to become a high school basketball coach. Clearly, my plan was not aligned with God's, as Mrs. Burrell returned in the middle of my sixth year of teaching and asked if I was ready to begin the process of becoming an administrator. By this time, I was frustrated with coaching and prepared for a new challenge. At the end of the year, Mrs. Burrell submitted my name for the program, and I was selected as one of the candidates to start the principal program. The program consisted of a full-year internship as an assistant principal while taking classes at the University of Texas at Arlington. I started the journey not truly understanding what it meant to lead adults, but I was confident in building positive relationships with kids. During my time as a classroom teacher and coach, I was very intentional about establishing a connection with my students. I would stand in the hallway during the passing periods and greet students with a handshake or a good morning. On days when other teachers would go to the teacher's lounge to eat, I would find myself hanging out in the cafeteria, engaging with the students. I would interact with the students during my before and after school duty. I knew their names and at least one thing about them. I found myself mentoring students, buying lunch for students who didn't have money, and listening to some of their struggles as teenagers.

Defining the Principal I Aspire to Be

If Webster's dictionary had a picture of the principal I aspired to be, it would be a picture of me smiling and interacting with students. If the dictionary had audio, you would hear me asking students about their weekend or talking to a student about the importance of choosing their friends wisely. I aspire to be the principal that students remember twenty to thirty years after they leave school. I focus on building positive relationships with all students by prioritizing their well-being, fostering trust and respect, and creating a supportive and inclusive school culture. Below is the mindset that drives my intentional interactions with my students.

The Blueprint

Student's First: I aspire to be the principal who will allow my students' needs, interests, and voices to guide my leadership, ensuring that the school culture is a place where all students feel valued and supported.

Easy to Find: I strive to be accessible and approachable to my students, making myself available for conversations, feedback, and support. I want all students to feel comfortable expressing their concerns, ideas, and aspirations.

Positive School Environment: I will create a positive and welcoming school culture where all students feel safe, respected, and included. The culture will be based on celebrating diversity, promoting empathy and kindness, and fostering a sense of belonging for all students.

Celebrate Student Success: I aspire to highlight students' achievements, talents, and contributions.

Student Voices: I will create a space for students to have a voice, as their ideas, opinions, and feedback are essential.

Encouraging Personal Growth: I will enable students to set goals, take on challenges, and strive for excellence.

Lifelong Impact: I aspire to be the principal who makes a positive and lasting impact on my students so that they carry the memories for the rest of their lives.

Building Positive Relationships

"We can't afford to wait 3 to 4 weeks into the school year to begin building positive relationships with our students. The process starts day 1."

Learning Students Names: The Power of Personal Connection

I've been in public education for 22 years, and it amazes me that I still remember the names of the students I interacted with at school. Whether it's through social media or running into a former student in the store, I can recall the student's name as if we were still at the same school. Usually, when I first meet a student, I will ask them their name, and each time I see the student throughout the building, I'm very intentional about calling them by either their first name or last. Sometimes, I don't remember, but I devise creative ways to get the students to tell me their names without them picking up that I forgot. It's essential for me as a principal to remember my students' names because it can yield many benefits.

Benefits of Learning Students Names

Sense of Belonging: When my students see that I know and remember their names, they feel they belong in the school, which can lead to increased student engagement and a more positive school environment.

Building Trust: Remembering my students' names demonstrates attentiveness and care on my part, and it helps to build trust between myself and the students. This connection can make students more comfortable approaching me when they have concerns or ideas.

Positive Relationships: Learning my students' names lays the foundation for a personal connection, which helps me build positive relationships with them. This can contribute to improved student behavior, as experience has taught me that students are more likely to respect authority figures with whom they feel connected at school.

Increased Motivation: Knowing my students' names can motivate them to excel academically and behaviorally. It creates a sense of accountability and encourages students to strive for success.

Enhanced Communication: When I make my students feel recognized and valued, they may be more open to communication. This can improve communication between myself and them, leading to improved collaboration and problem-solving.

As the principal, remembering the students' names can have far-reaching benefits. Students love it when we take the time to get to know them.

Finding Common Ground: Fostering Meaningful Conversations

The year after COVID-19 ended, I turned my vision of creating a mentoring program into a reality. For ten-plus years, I brainstormed ideas for creating a mentoring group for young men. I called the group IMPACT-1. The group aimed to equip young men with the necessary tools to go out into their community and the world and become "Difference Makers." When I think back to my time in middle and high school, we did not have access to a group of men outside our coaches who were willing to pour into us. Our coaches were great but tended to focus more on the sport than moving us from boys to men. Through IMPACT-1, I focused on giving young men essential life skills to turn them into future leaders.

IMPACT-1 Mentoring Model

PAC-1 Academy—Young men will be selected to go through an intense 9-month program. The focus will be on Essential Life Skills and other knowledge that will equip each young man with the skill set to go out and become "Difference Makers" in their community and the world.

I-Link – Designed to support each young man after he completes the PAC-1 Academy, we believe in "Lifelong Mentorship."

PAC-30—To build positive relationships with young men, IMPACT-1 will have lunch with small groups of young men to connect and hear from these young leaders. Each lunch segment will center on a central theme, a current issue the young men face, or one of the Essential Life Skills.

I-Serve—The goal of I-Serve is to make a positive impact on the lives of 25 or more young men between the ages of 8 and 18, to show them that someone cares, and to share life experiences that will lead them down the path to becoming "Difference Makers" within their community and throughout the world.

Each component of the model was good. However, the one that led us to meaningful conversations was PAC-30, as each meeting centered around a central theme. My schedule was busy as an assistant principal at the high school level, but I thought it was necessary to meet with the group of young men every Friday afternoon. During this semester, the United States was coming off a year of increased police shootings or killings of black men. The George Floyd case was one of the most notable cases during this time. After consulting with two teachers who helped me lead the group, we decided to use the subject of police shootings for our first PAC-30. On this day, we had a group of juniors and seniors who were a good mix of regular students and athletes. I had no idea how this would go, but these young men blew me away with how they were able to express themselves and have a healthy dialogue on the issue of police killings of black men. Within the discussion were points from both sides of the problem, but these young men did an excellent job respecting each other's opinions. Based on my experience in public education, there was no other platform within the school setting where these young men could have healthy dialogue about issues that were important to them.

We also engaged the young men in other conversations to help them change their thinking, which would hopefully change their behavior. During the years that I worked in the middle and high school setting, I noticed how our young men talked to and treated our young ladies. Immature comments and a focus on sex often characterize the typical interaction between a teenage boy and a teenage girl. On this Friday during PAC-30, we challenged the young men on how they treated the young women based on what we witnessed in the hallways and cafeteria, and we also gave them a blueprint on how to treat a lady. To help drive home our point, we had one of our female teachers stop by to speak to the group so they could hear it from the female perspective. The young men walked away from the session empowered and with a good understanding of the importance of respecting the ladies. Often, it takes a while to see the fruits of our labor, but at least we planted the seed in their hearts and minds.

Deeply Rooted: Mentorship

Growing up in Baton Rouge, LA, in the early 80s, I played youth sports, which laid the foundation for my passion for mentoring young men. My parents got my brother and me involved in youth sports from a very young age, and we participated in football and basketball until we started high school. I started playing organized football and basketball at the age of eight. During the fall, I played football with a youth organization called the Howell Park Cougars for seven straight years. We would practice Monday through Friday during the week and play games on Saturday mornings. When the winter and spring came, I transitioned to basketball with the Howell Park Sonics. During most years, some coaches and players from the Cougar organization were also a part of the Sonic organization. At the time, I didn't realize the sacrifice many of the coaches, my father included, were making to work with us. Most of these men worked full-time jobs and had families, but every evening during the week, they would show up to practice to prepare us for the games on Saturday mornings. More importantly, these were men of God, and I vividly remember praying side by side with my teammates at the end of each practice and before games. If you didn't know the Lord's Prayer, you had better learn it quickly because you never knew when it would be your time to pray.

    The men who coached us challenged us to be great athletes and great men. They were not afraid to hold us accountable and issue discipline when needed, but they showed us how to be compassionate and show grace. Many of us did not realize this then, but these chosen men were preparing us for life. In my case, those seven years of youth sports gave me the framework and the fuel to have a passion for mentoring young men. I remember every coach who ever engaged with me during this critical time, and I often remember the many lessons I learned. Let's take a walk down memory lane.

The Impact (Lessons Learned)

1. If you are early, you are on time; if you are on time, you are late.
2. You win as a team; you lose as a team.
3. Be willing to serve.
4. Don't be afraid to sacrifice to help someone else.
5. Pay attention to details.
6. Learn how to take constructive criticism/feedback.
7. It's ok to show emotions.
8. Always have your brother's back.
9. There is a time to lead, and there is a time to follow.
10. Family first

Meeting Students Where They Are: The Power of Mentoring / No Judgement

Over the last 22 years, I've had the opportunity to mentor hundreds of young men during my journey as an educator. Every year, I build positive relationships with young men who society has already counted out and labeled troublemakers. During the 2nd semester of the 2018-2019 school year, I had the pleasure of connecting with a young man named Phil, who was returning from an alternative school for possessing drugs on school grounds. When students return to school, we are notified by email of their return, so I added a reminder on my phone to meet with Phil upon his arrival at school.

On the morning of March 4, 2019, I saw Phil walk into the front office, so I met him. I aimed to greet the young man and let him know I was excited to see him back in school. I had no intention of bringing up his past challenges, as Phil's mistakes had been repeatedly mentioned over the past few months. After greeting him with a handshake, I cut to the chase and boldly told Phil that I needed him to graduate from high school. We briefly discussed the steps he needed to take to make graduation a reality, and I told him that I would be with him every step of the way.

After we shook hands again, and I was getting ready to walk back to my office, Phil turned around and said, "Mr. Anthony, I appreciate you." My brief interaction with this young man was a big deal. At no time in our conversation did I judge him or bring up the mistake he made. I welcomed him back and challenged him to finish high school.

To effectively mentor and speak into the lives of our students, we cannot begin the relationship by judging who they are on the surface. We can't honestly speak into their lives until we build positive relationships with them and earn their trust. Every day after meeting Phil, I intentionally made small deposits into our growing relationship until I gained his trust. I would randomly attend his class to see how he was doing. On other occasions, we would sit and have thought-provoking conversations about life—topics such as what it is like to be an African American male in America. During our discussions, I learned Phil was the only one working in his house. He sacrificed a lot to make sure he took care of his parents. I learned that Phil was shot in the face a few years earlier, and the bullet was lodged in his jaw. Phil uses it as a reminder that he wants to change his lifestyle. I learned that Phil wanted to go to college and start his own business despite the whispers from a society that said he would not make it. On May 31, 2019, Phil walked across the stage as a high school graduate. Thirty minutes before he walked across the stage, we briefly celebrated with a signature handshake that we came up with and a selfie. Phil may not remember my name 30 years from now, but he will remember the man who took the time to see his heart.

Cultivating a Culture of Belonging

"The message we communicate to our students daily plays a vital role in how they view school."

Making Every Student Feel Important

Over the years, I've intentionally made every student feel like they are the most important person in the room. One of my greatest fears of leaving the classroom to become a principal was losing the connection with the students. As a classroom teacher, you can form a special connection with each student in your class, a level of individual engagement that a principal, who oversees the entire student body, typically cannot achieve.

One example of me making my students feel important is when I worked at Lyles Middle School in Garland, Texas. Throughout the school year, I built individual relationships with all the 8th-grade students. I accomplished this by knowing their names and, more importantly, learning important information about them. Understanding who my students were on a personal level allowed me to write each of the two hundred 8th graders a personalized letter as a going-away gift as they transitioned to high school. It took me over a week to complete the task, but it was worth it. The students were shocked that I took the time to write each of them an encouraging letter crafted just for them. The gesture touched my heart two years later when I saw one of the students at a basketball game, and she stopped to tell me that she still had the handwritten letter hanging on her wall at home.

I continued spotlighting individual students when I arrived at Naaman Forest High School two years later. Around this time, I was reading Rich Dad, Poor Dad by Robert Kiyosaki, and we were discussing money management and investing during IMPACT-1 meetings. There was one young man named Roland, an excellent student who played football. During one of our conversations, he said he was interested in investing in the stock market and possibly real estate. Several essential factors in my relationship with Roland included my understanding of his interest in finances, so I surprised him with the book Rich Dad, Poor Dad. Roland was excited to get the book and was shocked that his principal would purchase the book for him. Because I knew Roland could not afford the book based on previous conversations, I took it upon myself to get it as a way of investing in his growth. When I returned to look at the picture we took of him holding the book, he felt like the most important person in the room. As a principal, making every student feel important is not just a goal but a fundamental aspect of creating a positive and inclusive school culture.

Authenticity Beyond the Title: Sharing Personal Stories

Often, the only side of us as principals that our students see is what society may consider the finished product. Our students see us in this season of life where we have already earned diplomas and degrees; to them, we are living our best lives. They don't see the struggles and challenges we went through to get to where we are today. I told my students I was not a finished product; I was still learning and growing like them. One of the strategies I use to build positive relationships with my students is to be authentic. I recall many times throughout my role as principal when I shared my personal story of overcoming the challenges of college.

When I first entered college, I needed to be more mentally focused to take on the many challenges that college would throw my way. I'm not saying that I could not perform academically at the college level, but my focus was not on studying; it was on playing basketball. During this time, I would eat, sleep, and drink basketball while my schoolwork and grades took a back seat. I worked on my skills in hopes of playing at the college level. My love for basketball was as intense as an addict's need for their next fix, and it completely drained my motivation to continue pursuing a college education. During my sophomore year, I stopped attending class, which affected my grades, and my school placed me on academic probation. I now had to find something productive to do during my suspension for one academic semester.

My grandfather owned his own construction business, and he allowed me to work with him on a few projects to keep me busy while I served my suspension. At first, we traveled to different jobs, working eight to nine hours a day, and that was fine with me because I was making money during the day and playing basketball every evening after I got off from work. Several weeks passed, and I was getting used to working to the point where I told myself, "I don't need school." I was a good enough worker to get a job at a company and work my way to the top. As I continued to think I could make it without an education, God stepped in and placed me in a life-changing situation. My grandfather took on a project that required him to build a facility for one of the sororities at Southern University, which would be constructed directly across the street from the campus. The new job location meant I would return to school in a different role. I got up every morning traveling the same path to work that I traveled to school, but I did not have a backpack full of books but a brown paper bag with a sandwich and chips for lunch. I worked with other men older than me who either dropped out of high school or finished high school but chose not to go to college. Analyzing these guys' every move, I realized I wanted more out of life. As I watched my brother's car pass the job site every morning en route to school, a little light bulb went off in my head about the importance of getting an education. As the sun beamed on my tired body as I picked up cement bags and sheetrock, I felt like a failure. As I went home each day after work covered in musk and dirt, I felt like I let my parents down. I then decided to return to school to continue my education, and I put any dreams of playing college basketball behind me. After enrolling back in school the following semester, I committed to passing every class with an A or B and graduating on the Dean's List. When I stepped onto the campus and entered my first class, I felt like I had been born a new man.

My hunger for knowledge and to succeed was off the charts. While other students went to the student union to take a break between classes, I went to the library's top floor to read books on various subjects and think about life. Some days, I would sit by the window and look into the blue skies, dreaming of making a difference in the world. I discovered this new appreciation for education, which helped me graduate from college with a degree in secondary education, and I accomplished my goal of graduating on the dean's list. As I sit back and think about my struggle, I thank God that I experienced the things that I did. God had a plan for my life that consisted of me dropping out of school, re-enrolling in school, and finally graduating from school. I spent ten years in college. Some people may find something wrong because the average time to finish a bachelor's Degree is 4 to 5 years. I'm thankful that I spent 10 years in college. It allowed me to discover my purpose in life and prepared me to fulfill my purpose of making a difference in students' lives.

Nurturing Growth and Accountability

"A positive school culture is the foundation for student success."

Holding Students Accountable: Balancing Support and Expectations

I was born and raised in Baton Rouge, LA, so I was used to seeing or hearing about the damage that a hurricane can bring to an area. In August of my senior year of high school, we experienced Hurricane Andrew, a powerful category-five storm that struck Louisiana. We were without lights for a few days but fortunately, we had enough food and water to last until the lights came back. As kids, we made the best of the situation by hanging out in the neighborhood and playing with family and friends. Fast forward 13 years later, and the kids in New Orleans who experienced Hurricane Katrina were not as lucky as us. Some of these kids lost their homes and family members, with a large percentage being uprooted and dispersed throughout the country.

In the fall of 2005, we received a group of students at my school who moved to Texas after Hurricane Katrina. The transition was difficult as these students left everything they had ever known in New Orleans. Upon arriving on campus, the New Orleans students immediately went into survival mode to assert themselves and demonstrate to the Texas students that they were tough. This caused turmoil on campus daily as both groups were fighting for dominance. We had several fights within the first few weeks, but the one that stuck out the most was in the school cafeteria. This situation turned dangerous quickly as two large groups engaged in a physical altercation, with chairs and tables being thrown throughout the cafeteria. We were able to get the fight under control with no significant injuries, but holding the students accountable and supporting them was the real challenge.

After the cafeteria altercation, we faced a decision. Although the students involved in the fight needed to face the consequences, it was crucial to consider all factors and find ways to support both groups, particularly the New Orleans students who had lost everything. Here are a few reasons why it was essential to hold them accountable but also give them support:

Accountability & Support Essentials

Maintaining Excellence: Holding students accountable reinforces behavior expectations, ensuring clarity on boundaries and consequences.

Growth Through Errors: Accountability enables students to understand the impact of their actions, fostering better choices in the future.

Fostering Development: Supporting students while holding them accountable encourages personal development and resilience, emphasizing that mistakes are opportunities for learning and growth.

Trust Building: Fair and consistent accountability fosters trust between students and educators, which is vital for a positive learning environment.

Root Cause Analysis: Supporting accountability helps educators identify and tackle underlying issues, aiding students' academic and social success.

Cultivating Belonging: Accountability measures that support students foster a sense of community, positively influencing their well-being and academic performance.

Future Readiness: Teaching accountability and providing support equips students with skills and resilience for academic and professional challenges ahead.

High Fives, Fist Bumps, and Hugs: Creating a Culture of Affirmation

As a school Principal, my interactions with students extend far beyond the confines of the classroom. Whether walking down the halls, entering classrooms, or waiting in the carpool line, each moment presents an opportunity to connect with my students on a personal level. Here's how the simple acts of high fives, fist bumps, and hugs contribute to nurturing a culture of affirmation within my school building:

Engaging Intentionally

Every interaction with a student is a chance to make them feel valued and appreciated. When I walk through the building, I am deliberate about greeting students and making each one feel like the most critical person in the world. This intentional engagement sets the tone for positive relationships and a supportive learning environment.

Tailoring Interactions

One size does not fit all when interacting with my students. My interactions may vary depending on the individual and the relationship I've cultivated with them. For some students, a high five is a simple yet meaningful acknowledgment of their presence. Others may prefer a fist bump, conveying camaraderie and solidarity. And then there are moments when a warm hug is needed to provide comfort and reassurance.

Reading Emotional Cues

The key to effective engagement lies in reading my students' emotions. Each interaction is an opportunity to gauge their mood and respond accordingly. By paying attention to subtle cues such as body language and facial expressions, I can tailor my gestures to meet their emotional needs. Some days, a student may need extra encouragement and support, signaling that a hug may be more appropriate than a fist bump.

Fostering Connection

High fives, fist bumps, and hugs are more than just physical gestures – they are powerful tools for building connections and fostering a sense of belonging. These simple acts of affirmation tell students they are seen, heard, and valued in our school community. By consistently offering these gestures of support, I create a culture where kindness, empathy, and inclusivity thrive.

Empowering Through Support

"Two questions to ask at the end of the school day:

1. *Did I help my students grow today?*
2. *Did I improve myself today?"*

Small Group Lunches: Creating Safe Spaces for Dialogue

As I reflect on my school days, I don't recall seeing my principals sit down and have lunch with the students. Typically, the principals were on duty in the cafeteria, watching to ensure we were behaving, and no food fights took place. As a principal, I discovered that lunch is one of the most critical times for building positive relationships with my students. As an administrator at a junior high school, I started bringing my lunch to the cafeteria and sitting at the table eating with the kids. The kids loved it, and on a few occasions, different tables were mad at the other table because they wanted me to eat with them.

Honestly, I had no set talking points, and often, I would sit and listen to the kids be kids. When I did talk, I engaged the students in topics that interested them, but once I earned their trust, I began including topics they could learn and benefit from. As I became more strategic, I started selecting random groups of students to have lunch with in the school conference room. The change allowed me to get to know different students and choose a different topic to discuss during the 30-minute lunch break. My lunch group began to spread throughout the school, and before I knew it, I would have random students showing up in the front office requesting lunch with me. There were many days when I was working on a task in my office, and I looked up only to see multiple kids speed-walking toward my door to have lunch. How could I tell them no, even though I was super busy? It taught me to take a break as the work would be there.

Three Benefits of Having Lunch with My Kids

Building Stronger Relationships

Sitting down for lunch with my students allows me to build stronger, more personal relationships. It shows students that I am approachable and interested in their lives beyond academic performance, fostering a sense of trust and connection.

Gaining Insights into Student Life

Lunch conversations provide me with valuable insights into student concerns, interests, and the overall school climate. This firsthand understanding helps make informed decisions that better address the needs and well-being of the student body.

Creating a Positive School Culture

When I regularly interact with students during lunch, it helps create a welcoming and inclusive school culture. Students feel valued and respected, leading to increased morale, improved behavior and a stronger sense of community within the school.

Filling in the Gaps: Supporting Basic Needs

Over my years as a principal, I have lost count of how many times I've bought a student lunch, given them a few dollars, or bought them a coat during winter. There was one particular student who moved to Texas right after Hurricane Katrina. I remember him coming to school each day during the winter months with no coat and wearing a short-sleeved shirt. One day, I asked if he had a coat at home, and he said yes, but he didn't like wearing one. I later discovered that he didn't have a coat and only said he did because he was embarrassed. Without a second thought, I went home that night and picked out one of my favorite coats to give to him. When I arrived at school the next day and surprised him with the coat, he had tears in his eyes. He thanked me and wore the jacket every day afterward. I will never forget this young man, whose life was tragically cut short by a bullet after he and a friend were playing with a loaded gun.

Stories like these show the importance of supporting our students' basic needs. By addressing these needs, we help them succeed academically and show them that they are valued and cared for.

Leading with Compassion: Advocating for Every Student

I've seen firsthand that not every student who walks through the doors of a school has someone at home to advocate for them. Each school I've worked at has presented opportunities to support and fight for students in need. One particular day stands out vividly in my memory. A group of students fought during a pep rally at a high school where I was working. After we managed to bring them to the office, I started processing paperwork for a student named Emmanuel. Emmanuel, or Manny as he was known, was a tough young man with the fighting skills to back it up. He straddled a fine line between the streets and the potential for greatness. As I processed his suspension papers, I looked closer at his academic records and discovered he was knowledgeable and part of the STEM program.

When his mother arrived to pick him up, we had a long conversation about Emmanuel and his path. Despite raising him in a loving home, she explained that she was struggling against the pull of the neighborhood gang, which had Emmanuel's full attention. He was caught in a challenging situation, torn between wanting to please his mother and maintaining street credibility with his friends. I will never forget his mother's plea: "Mr. Anthony, please save my son." From that moment, I became Emmanuel's most ardent advocate. I met with him regularly throughout the week to ensure he stayed on top of his academics.

Additionally, I served as a buffer between him and a rival gang that wanted to hurt him. Thanks to the positive relationships I had built with both groups, they respected my wishes enough to avoid fighting at school. However, controlling their actions outside of school was another matter entirely.

Tragically, the summer before his junior year, Emmanuel lost his best friend to gun violence. Emmanuel held his friend in his arms as he died, an event that profoundly affected him.

I noticed a significant change in Emmanuel afterward; he seemed determined to make better choices. I continued to work closely with him until his family moved, necessitating a transfer to a new school. Fortunately, I maintained contact with Emmanuel through his siblings, who remained at our school.

Today, I still follow Emmanuel from a distance via social media. He has channeled his energy into a promising boxing career, and I am proud to see his strides. Emmanuel's journey is a powerful reminder of the impact we can have when we advocate for our students and support them through their most demanding challenges.

Making Connections: The Blueprint

Carpool Line

"The carpool line can be challenging, but it's rewarding. The look on their faces when I open the car door and greet them each morning is priceless."

Carpool Line

Be available in the mornings and afternoons to greet students as they arrive and depart from school. This is an excellent opportunity to get to know your students and their parents. Treat the morning arrival like a five-star hotel by opening the door for students and greeting them with a cheerful "Good Morning." Being present in the carpool line allows us to gauge how our students are feeling. If you notice a student is upset or not acting like themselves, take the time to check in with them before the school day begins. Additionally, being present in the carpool line provides a chance to interact with parents.

Carpool Line Rhythms

Carpool Corner - Make a deliberate effort to give genuine compliments to students as they arrive or depart each day. This simple act can significantly boost their confidence and improve their mood.

Celebration Spotlight - Share positive news with parents about their child when they arrive to pick them up from school.

Lunch Time Chats

"Who will you inspire today? Step off the sidelines and dive into the game of youth mentoring."

Lunch Time Chats

As a principal, carving out time to have lunch with your students is critical to building and maintaining positive relationships with them. This shared time allows for informal interactions, fostering community and trust. It offers a unique opportunity to understand students' perspectives, address their concerns, and celebrate their achievements in a relaxed setting. By prioritizing these moments, you demonstrate genuine care and interest in their well-being, which can significantly enhance their school experience and create a more inclusive and supportive school environment.

Lunch Time Rhythms

Talk It Out Fridays - Choose different tables each Friday to engage in casual conversations, getting to know students' interests and hobbies.

Power 30: Invite small groups of students to have lunch with you in a designated area. This will allow for more personal and meaningful interactions.

Student Recognitions - During lunch, acknowledge and celebrate student achievements or good deeds over the intercom, creating a positive and inclusive atmosphere.

Classroom Visits

"Always make time to celebrate your accomplishments, whether big or small."

Classroom Visits

As principals, our role in the learning environment is to evaluate teachers, but it also allows us to engage actively with our students. This practice not only demonstrates your genuine interest in their educational journey but also allows you to connect with them on a deeper level. These visits provide a unique opportunity to observe their progress, understand their challenges, and even teach a lesson or two. Students appreciate and enjoy having the principal step into the role of their teacher for the day, as it adds variety to their routine and shows that their leaders are actively engaged in their education. Such interactions foster a stronger, more supportive school community.

Classroom Visit Rhythms

Random Visits - Occasionally visit classrooms unannounced with a fun story or activity to share, making your presence exciting and welcoming.

Learning Walks - Participate in lessons or activities, showing genuine interest in students' learning and doing.

Feedback Fridays: Offer to spend a few minutes in each classroom on Fridays providing positive feedback and encouragement to students and teachers.

Hallway Super Star

"It's a great day to go out and be amazing."

Hallway Super Star

It's cool and fun for principals to interact with students in the hallway. These casual, spontaneous encounters break down barriers, making the principal more approachable and relatable. By engaging with students in this informal setting, principals can share their day-to-day experiences, offer encouragement, and address any immediate concerns. These interactions lighten the atmosphere and build a stronger sense of community and trust within the school. Students feel valued and understood, knowing their principal takes an active interest in their school life beyond the classroom.

Hallway Rhythms

Positive Post-Its: Leave encouraging notes on lockers or desks, recognizing students' efforts and achievements.

Super Star Spotlights - Create a bulletin board in the hallway to highlight student successes, projects, or acts of kindness.

Hallway Helpers- Acknowledge and reward students who demonstrate positive behavior in the hallways, reinforcing respectful and responsible actions.

A Recess to Remember

"Oftentimes, we don't see the impact we have on young people until years later. The key is to plant the seed."

A Recess to Remember

A school principal hanging out with students during recess can profoundly impact the school community. This informal interaction allows the principal to connect with students in a relaxed and playful environment, fostering positive relationships and building trust. The principal demonstrates genuine interest in students' lives beyond academics by engaging in games, conversations, or simply being present. This presence can also serve as an opportunity to observe social dynamics, address issues in real time, and promote a culture of inclusivity and support. The principal's involvement during recess helps create a more cohesive and caring school environment.

Recess Rhythms

Principal's Play Day: Join students during recess for games and activities, showing your playful and approachable side.

Recess Challenges: To foster teamwork and excitement, organize fun challenges or competitions, such as a relay race or scavenger hunt.

Recess Reflections: Spend the last few minutes of recess chatting with students about their day, making connections, and showing them, you care.

Support Outside of School

"Push excuses aside. Your purpose is greater than any excuse. Get it done."

Support Outside of School

Principals supporting their students outside school can be incredibly important for building positive relationships. Attending extracurricular activities, such as sports events, school plays, or community service projects, shows students that their principal cares about their interests and achievements beyond the classroom. This involvement fosters a sense of connection and respect, making students feel valued and understood. When principals actively participate in their student's lives, they reinforce a supportive school culture and demonstrate a commitment to the holistic development of their students. This external support can significantly enhance the principal-student relationship, contributing to a more engaged and motivated student body.

Outside of School Rhythms

Community Events - Attend and support school-related community events like sports games, performances, or science fairs, showing students you are interested in their lives outside school.

Family Events: Host monthly events inviting families to the school for fun activities, fostering a stronger school-community relationship.

Home Visits - Schedule home visits for students needing extra support, creating a personal and caring connection.

Building Lifelong Relationships

Youth mentorship is deeply important to me, and this group of young men from Berkner High School was my first set of mentees. We took a trip to the University of Texas at Dallas for a symposium dedicated to African American boys. One of the best moments from the trip was lunch as we got a chance to sit and talk about the many things that we face as African American men, and how we can continue to strive for excellence.

As we interact with our students, they often become like our own children. I met Jeremiah Williams when he was a 7th grader in junior high school. He was an excellent student and a talented athlete. Jeremiah went on to win a state football championship in high school and later played college football while earning his degree. Today, he works in education and is passionate about mentoring youth.

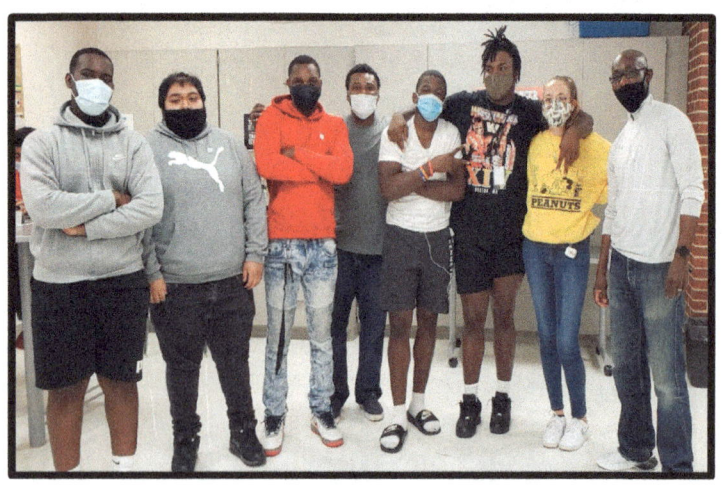

During COVID, our lives changed forever, but my dedication to mentoring and building positive relationships with young men remained unwavering. Upon returning to school after the shutdown, I established the Impact-1 mentoring program at Naaman Forest High School. We truly made a significant impact on the lives of the young men we worked with during that challenging time.

Through Impact 1 Mentoring, I met with a group of male students every Friday to discuss topics and issues important to them and us as men. This process was called Pac-30. On one day, we discussed the impact of police shootings on our community, as this meeting took place in the fall after George Floyd's death. The group did an incredible job addressing the issue from both perspectives. The students had never experienced a group where they could express themselves freely without judgment. I vividly remember one senior student, Tommy Dunn, saying, "Where was this group my freshman year?" Our students seek mentors and guidance, and we must create a space for them.

I first met Jamie Stewart when she was in junior high school. She was an exceptionally talented young lady and an outstanding student. I reconnected with Jamie at a job fair in my district, unaware that she was now a teacher there as well. It's an incredible feeling to see a former student follow the same career path and remember the positive interactions we had when she was my student.

"Mr. Anthony, is that you?" Anytime I hear that phrase, I get excited because it's usually from a former student. Shemecia Lewis, who was one of my students in junior high school, approached me at an elementary basketball game at her kids' school. We reminisced about all the fun times from her 8th-grade year, and she thanked me for always "keeping it real" with her and her classmates. The positive connections we build with our students last a lifetime.

I was shopping with my family when a young man approached me and said, "I think you were my principal." I jokingly replied, "I think I was your principal." Then I said, "Christian, is that you?" His eyes lit up when he realized I remembered his name. Christian and I had many interactions during his junior high school years, and we shared a brief laugh about the times he got into trouble. During our conversation, he thanked me for holding him accountable.

I will never forget the face of a former student. One Sunday morning, as church service was ending, I looked across the sanctuary and noticed Matthew, whom I taught and coached in 7th and 8th grade. Seeing this young man in church with his wife and kids was beautiful. It was gratifying to hear about all the great things he has accomplished so far.

I met Joel when he was a junior in high school, and he was part of my mentoring group in his junior and senior years. After his senior year, I switched school districts and moved to a different school. One day, I was sitting in my office when the secretary called and said, "Mr. Anthony, you have a former student here to see you." I was shocked, as I hadn't shared my move with many people. As I walked around the corner, to my surprise, it was Joel. He was headed Texas Tech and wanted to see me before starting his college journey. He told me he searched the internet and asked around the city to find out where I was because he needed to talk to me before leaving for school. It speaks volumes when former students come looking for you.

Initially, it took me a moment to adjust to working with the children of former students. It made me feel like I was getting old, but it's truly a blessing to have the opportunity to impact families across generations. I worked with this young lady when she was in junior high school, and many years later, I became the elementary principal for her two daughters. Her oldest daughter was always curious about her mom as a student, asking me many questions. This helped us build a positive relationship throughout the year.

Former students are thrilled to come back to their old school and share positive updates about their lives. This young man used to be part of the group I mentored when he was in high school. I always knew he was destined for success because he was diligent in his studies and excelled as a football player.

While working with students, we often don't realize the influence we have on them. Trey Stewart, one of my players from junior high school, is now a teacher and coach, impacting the lives of the next generation. During our conversation, he thanked me for positively influencing his life and inspiring him to become an educator. I am incredibly proud of Trey and his growth as a young man, and I was thrilled to see him be part of a state basketball championship as a high school coach. Before becoming a principal, one of my goals was to coach high school basketball and win a state championship. Although I chose a different path, I feel like I accomplished that goal through Trey.

Each year since I have become a principal, I've been blessed to work with the siblings or children of my former students. I worked with this young lady when she was in high school, and I got the chance to become her son's elementary principal. Principals working with the children of former students often find it a rewarding experience that bridges generations. It's a unique opportunity to continue influencing the same families, building on past relationships and fostering new ones. These connections can create a deeper sense of community and continuity, as the principal's positive impact on the parents is remembered and extended to their children. This dynamic not only strengthens the school environment but also highlights the enduring legacy of a principal's dedication to education and mentorship.

A few years ago, my family and I purchased a home in a different city from where we work. After long days at work, my wife and I would take walks in the neighborhood to unwind. One evening, after returning from a walk, I received a Facebook message from Willie Woods, a former student. He wrote, "Mr. Anthony, I'm not sure it was you, but I saw a guy walking in my neighborhood who looked just like you." I laughed and replied, "That guy was me." A few months later, we ran into each other at the grocery store and had a chance to catch up and reminisce about his time in junior high school. I also got to meet his two boys. It's a wonderful feeling to see former male students as fathers and husbands.

Several mornings before work, I stop at the gas station near my house to fuel up or grab a few snacks for the day. One morning, while pumping gas, I heard, "Mr. Anthony, is that you?" It was still dark outside, so I couldn't see the person's face, but the voice sounded familiar. It turned out to be Devin Smith, one of my former students. Each year, there's always one student who is more mature than his age, and Devin was that guy. I fondly remember our great conversations and laughs in the cafeteria, hallways, and on the football field. I spoke with him almost every day during junior high, as we shared a connection being both from Louisiana. This interaction made my day and inspired me to keep striving to become the principal I never had.

Throughout my educational journey, running into former students always brings overwhelming joy. In this photo, I reconnected with Courtney Smith, one of my former student-athletes, at a marriage conference. I hadn't seen him since his 8th-grade year. It brought back memories of conversations about respect, honesty, accountability, hard work, setbacks, winning and losing, peer pressure, and more. These young men remember the intentional talks about decision-making and respecting women. They recall my personal stories, like flunking out of college with a 1.9

GPA but returning to graduate on the Dean's List. They remember me waiting patiently after practice until their parents arrived because I wanted to ensure they made it home safely. It's the small things that count.

My wife and I headed out for a date night at one of our favorite restaurants. When we arrived and pulled into the parking lot, I saw one of the valet attendants walking towards our car, ready to park it as we entered. To my surprise, the valet attendant was Desmond Shorter, one of my former students. Despite having reservations at a specific time, Desmond and I talked for nearly twenty minutes, catching up on old times. I also had the privilege of working with his older brother, John Shorter, a student at our school.

Meet Philip, the young man I mentioned earlier in the book. I first met him when he returned to school after making an unwise choice. I worked with Philip for the remainder of his senior year, promising to ensure he graduated. This picture represents the power of not judging students who make mistakes but instead becoming advocates for them and helping them achieve their goals. I have never given up on a student in my twenty-two years in education.

Who says you can't overcome life's obstacles? Life may throw you curveballs, but you must keep swinging. This young man will have a compelling testimony because he never gave up. I will always cherish this moment, as I can still hear his voice saying, "Mr. Anthony, thank you for believing in me."

I met Rafael years ago when he moved to Texas from Louisiana after Hurricane Katrina as a junior high student. I shared a unique bond with my New Orleans students in 2005, as Louisiana was also my home. We connected over stories of Gumbo, King Cake, Crawfish, and catching beads during Mardi Gras. While the Texas kids laughed at how the Louisiana kids pronounce their words, I encouraged the New Orleans students to be themselves despite others' opinions. I challenged my Texas students to embrace the differences their new classmates brought and to understand the pain and trauma the New Orleans students carried after losing everything.

I met Jalen Broussard after he and his family moved to Texas from New Orleans after Hurricane Katrina. He was a great student and excelled in football and basketball. He is currently working on his degree at the University of North Texas.

As a principal, it's always thrilling to witness graduates crossing the stage. On this memorable night, it was particularly special—I had the honor of presenting my own son with his high school diploma. An incredible and deeply personal moment.

Shattered Dreams

I almost didn't become a principal. At the end of my second year as an Assistant Principal, my principal left for a central office position. To close out the 2011 school year and begin planning for the next, I was named interim principal. I believed I was ready to step up and lead a school, so I applied for the head principal position. I was eager, hopeful, and convinced that this was the next step in my journey.

A few weeks passed, and I still hadn't heard anything from Human Resources regarding my application for the principal position. As summer neared its end and the school year approached, it was time for administrators to attend the annual summer leadership conference. I vividly remember sitting at a table during the meeting when the Area Superintendent of Secondary Schools approached me and asked if I could step into another room. As I rose from the table, excitement and nervousness swept over me. The only thought in my mind was that I was about to transition from interim principal to principal. I noticed two other central administrators seated at the table when I entered the room. The conversation began with the Area Superintendent thanking me for my excellent work as interim principal. However, he then explained that I would not be considered for an interview for the head principal position. He was straightforward and said he didn't want me to go through the interview process, knowing I wouldn't be selected. I left that room wholly crushed.

The blow was more than just a professional setback; it was personal. I lost confidence in myself, and my once-clear aspiration to become a principal faded into the background. That single meeting altered my path for over a decade. Despite encouragement from colleagues and mentors to apply for open principal positions, I refused. The pain of that rejection and the fear of reliving that experience kept me from pursuing the role I once dreamed of. For 12 long years, I avoided any opportunity to become a head principal. The wound from that meeting never truly healed—it scarred over, making me doubt my capabilities and question whether I was meant to lead.

The Blessing in Disguise

Reflecting on not being selected for the principalship in 2011, I realize how thankful I am for that setback. It felt like a crushing blow at the time, but today, I see it as one of the most critical moments in my career.

I'm grateful for the honesty of those in that room who had the difficult task of telling me I wasn't ready. I remember one saying, *"Once you move forward, there is no turning back."* That statement resonated with me, though I didn't fully appreciate its wisdom then. Staying as an Assistant Principal for those additional years gave me the chance to hone my skills, deepen my understanding of school leadership, and, most importantly, impact the lives of countless students. Thinking about what I would have missed had I moved into a principalship too soon makes me cringe. The relationships I built, the lives I touched, and the lessons

I learned as an AP were invaluable. What once seemed like a door closing was a window opening, allowing me to become the leader I am today.

The Final Bell

"Becoming the principal I never had means embodying the mentor, leader, and advocate I once needed. It's about creating an environment where every student feels seen, heard, and inspired to reach their full potential, knowing that someone believes in them every step of the way."

The Final Bell

Reflecting on my journey of becoming the principal I never had, I think about the countless individuals who shaped me. From the mentors who guided me to the students who inspired me, each interaction left an indelible mark on my leadership style and understanding of empathy. Becoming the principal I never had was not just about filling a void from my past; it was about creating a space where every student felt seen, heard, and valued. It meant leading with empathy and understanding that behind every disciplinary issue or academic struggle was a human being with a story, hopes, and dreams.

Throughout my tenure as principal, I faced numerous challenges and triumphs. There were days when the weight of responsibility felt overwhelming, and moments of doubt crept in. But during those times, I leaned on the lessons I had learned from my own experiences and the remarkable individuals who had crossed my path. One of the most profound lessons I learned was the power of relationships. Building strong connections with my students became the cornerstone of my leadership philosophy. I prioritized fostering a trust, collaboration, and respect culture where all students felt empowered to contribute their ideas and talents.

Empowering my students to reach their full potential became my driving force. I strived to create opportunities for growth and development through mentorship. By investing in the growth of my students, I witnessed remarkable transformations in both individuals and the school community. The most rewarding aspect of my journey was seeing my efforts impact my students' lives. From Emmanuel, who defied the odds to pursue his passion for boxing, to countless others who found their voice, purpose, and path to success, each success story reinforced my belief in the transformative power of education.

As I pen the concluding chapter of this book, I'm filled with gratitude for the privilege of serving as a principal. My journey has been one of continuous growth, learning, and evolution. But above all, it has been a journey of empathy, leadership, and transformation. I extend my deepest thanks to all who have accompanied me on this journey—my mentors, colleagues, students, and family members. I hope I have redefined what it means to lead with empathy, inspire purposefully, and transform lives through education. May this book serve as a testament to the incredible potential within each of us to make a difference in the lives of others. May it inspire future generations of principals and leaders to embrace empathy, lead with compassion, and strive for excellence in all they do.

"He may not remember my name, but he will remember the man who took the time to make him feel like the most important person in the room."

Made in the USA
Coppell, TX
07 October 2024